Why We Do Our Daily Practices

Dale Biron

 PACK MULE PRESS

Some of these poems originally appeared on the Gratefulness and
A Few Wild Stanzas websites and in *Animus Journal*.
    www.gratefulness.org: "Gratefulness" and "Laughter"
    www.afewwildstanzas.com: "The Hawk Is Like the Heart,"
                            "Follow Your Weird" and
                            "I Do Not Want To Be a Good Leader"
    Animus Journal: "On the Occasion of Speaking Out Against Rarefied Poetry"

Editing and book design by Jo Anne Smith
Cover by Dale Biron

Printed in the United States of America

ISBN 978-0-9912889-0-8

For

Judy Burgio

CONTENTS

QUOTES ABOUT POETRY TO WHICH I ASPIRE ...

As you read these poems, if even one reaches the heights of these quotes, I will feel a deep sense of satisfaction and joy. Some are my own guides, others are attributed:

- *Poems should work for a living, with gifts for the heart, head and hara (aka gut).*

- *Poems are bifocals for the soul.*

- *If the poet can hold the thread lightly enough, make their gaze soft enough, pick up the slightest scents, then they can't help but cohere into some truth.*

- *You would be surprised at how many leaders use poetry to stay grounded and inspired. For them poetry never left the building.*

- *Great poetry should survive on its own in any kind of weather and not simply in the hothouse environment of the English or literature classroom.*

- *Great poems trust and invite the reader or listener inside the words to have their own unique and personal experience.*

- *Great poetry has a sensitive BS Meter that goes off at the slightest detection.*

- *Poems begin in delight and end in wisdom.* – Robert Frost

- *Poetry: Language against which we have no defense.* – David Whyte

- *Stories change us; they change the world. People are stories of themselves.* – Karen Healey

- *I gave up science for poetry because poetry was so much more precise.* – David Whyte

- *Poetry is the music of the soul, and, above all, of great and feeling souls.* – Voltaire

- *A poem is compressed thought, intense and clear as diamonds.* – Stephen Spender

- *One thing about great art, it made you love people more, forgive them their petty transgressions. It worked in the way that religion was supposed to.* – Nick Hornby

- *In a sense, poems are not even fair. For instance, they do not always assert what they mean.* – William Stafford

MY PATH TO POETRY

So many of us have had perfect storms arrive in our lives. I was no different. For me, it was my mid-thirties when the first big losses came crashing into my life. My mother died. My marriage ended. My company fell apart. I had the image of falling down a dark mine shaft backwards with nothing to grab on to or break my fall. It was scary. It was devastating. For over a year all I could manage was a kind of limping from one day to the next. The saying, "This too shall pass" seemed like a big fat lie!

It wasn't. Things did began to shift. Clouds dispersed and the sun eventually arrived.

For each thing that had left, something new arrived. After having my own computer software business and running a national sales effort, I started over again as a trainee. I studied everything I could get my hands on that pertained to this new vocation. I became a "beginner's mind" neophyte in the business of coaching and consulting. I joined a Toastmasters group and began public speaking. At Toastmasters I met the person who would become my new business partner and soulmate.

The next year I was introduced to a very strange martial art called Aikido. Its practices and rules taught reconciliation rather than violence. It trained and advocated for a reduction of aggression rather than simply meeting it with bigger and better violence. It was the start of a ten-year journey to a black belt in this art.

The changes in my life were not yet done. At a public event in Nevada City only months after I began to practice Aikido, I heard the clarion call of an art that was to become my obsession.

The presenter quoted these few stunning words from a long poem entitled "Asphodel, That Greeny Flower" by William Carlos Williams ...

My heart rouses
> *thinking to bring you news*
>> *of something*

that concerns you
> *and concerns many men. Look at*
>> *what passes for the new.*

You will not find it there but in
> *despised poems.*
>> *It is difficult*

to get the news from poems
> *yet men die miserably every day*
>> *for lack*

of what is found there.

The speaker of those words? Amazing poet and teacher, David Whyte. For me it was a hopeless case of adult poetry-onset disease. Since then I've never stopped reading, speaking about and writing poetry. Of course it's the genesis of this book of poems.

A VERY BRIEF INTRODUCTION

"You can't force a poem to do anything it doesn't want to do, but if it decides to do something, you can't stop it either." – Dale Biron

I have never been able to cure myself from a feeling that good poetry is practical and useful. Like William Stafford used to say, poems are just stories without the boring parts.

This has become my thing, as they say. It has become my thing because I want it to be. Because like all the other humans on this planet, I believe it so I then look to prove it. Does that mean it is not true? Yes and no. It all depends upon how I feel.

Yes, the feeling comes first. You see my way of writing is to begin by not writing. I actually read other things, other poems, other quotes. I call it the "Ricochet Method."

How it works? A thread emerges. A snippet of a feeling comes. I stop the internal chatter as best I can. (This is not easy, have you noticed?) I then soften my gaze and just start writing. Not fast, but not slow either. I try to hold everything lightly the way I was taught to practice the martial art of Aikido. My teacher would say, have soft gaze. Focus on nothing so that you can see everything.

The worst part! In writing poetry like practicing Aikido, you can't try. Trying is the surest route to bad poetry and bad Aikido. But wait, wasn't I taught to be a hard-driving and conscientious worker bee until I achieved my goals? Yes I was. And with some things it works well, but with art ... not so much. So, I need to use all that discipline to put the pen in my hand daily. Or whatever it is that I need – aka love – to log 10,000 hours of doing it.

15

Then, as they say in jazz ... I forget all that technical stuff and just wail!

And that's my invitation to you ... just step inside each poem and enjoy!

WHY WE DO OUR DAILY PRACTICES

Some days you will simply feel off,
shut down from the start or maybe
by a dream stuttering or ending.
Or when a good plan just falters.

It is great comfort then to have
things to do, practices to keep,
journals to write and share or not.
The feeling now is so dense.

Some darkness has you cornered:
scared, frozen or turned to molten fire.
Next moment and the next, just watch:
Change will come. Sunlight happens.

LAUGHTER

When the
face we wear

grows old and weathered, torn
open by time,

colors
tinted as dawn

like the late
winter mountains

of Sedona
ashen and crimson.

It will no longer
be possible

to distinguish
our deepest scars

from the long
sweet lines left

by laughter.

ON THE OCCASION OF SPEAKING OUT
AGAINST RAREFIED POETRY

for Judy

OK, OK, all right. I'll tell you this much -
It's high time poetry came tumbling down
To the crowds, to the folks I mean.
Ask me? What kind of poetry I would
Like to see in this world? Right, well imagine
A super market, the checkout man I mean,
Those thick, stubby fingers, a wedding ring
Swollen on permanent, skin thickened by hard work
Handling the groceries of thousands, reaching
For a pack of poems, right beside the razor
Blades and the cigarettes and I don't smoke either,
But the people that do smoke need
Poems just as much as me. Yes, I want
Practical, hard working, truck-horse poems,
In this world, and ads for those
Poems too right along side the Kleenex, and the Ajax
That fill those Thursday flyers in the daily paper.
I want to see a holiday sale on William Stafford,
Yeats maybe, Mary Oliver and that fierce German,
Rilke. I want to see the CEO of Exxon
Quote Emily Dickinson in the Annual Report!
And of course in schools too, I want poetry
Vending machines, where the real thing
Isn't sweet syrupy water, its Rumi. I want
To see scalpers working the stadium where

A football game has been cancelled for lack of
Interest, yelling, "Yo! Seamus Heaney, Wendell Berry,
Yehuda Amichai, right here, two good seats left folks."
I want to see MTV break all those rating records
On the night they feature Anna Akhmatova.
I want to see CSPAN cover the annual convention
Of ex-congress members who are now active poets.
But most of all, and I mean most of all, its this:
I want to turn to you stunned, my mate-women, on
Any old average, candle-lit night and touching the softness that is
your body just before making love and say to us: My God! Neruda
was right, "Sometimes a piece of sun burns like a coin in my
hand" when I realize how much I love you.

THE HARBORING ORGANIZATIONS

All the organizations that harbor
soul-less, stressed out jobs
are the ships,

Poet-coaches the
lifeboats.

Every sane person I know has
jumped overboard.

That is good for business
isn't it

Dale?

LIGHT SWITCH

Flipping on the bathroom light this morning
each watt emanating from behind the
white frosted glass, I felt a sudden surge
and began to think how wires connect things,
heaving houses pulsing with nerves
that mimic our bodies that mimic the heavens.

The way they connect to larger wires
arching out through enormous expanses of air
toward the great roadside timbers fitted with coats
of creosote to press the bugs into service elsewhere.

And back and back to the great steel
towers standing watch over desserts,
forests, hills, vast prairies that have seen
civilizations grind themselves slowly away.

And mountains filled with ancient snow,
mountains made from volcanoes, earthquakes
and the great tectonic plates shifting below
and that snow too that became water
and that water that became river
that turned the great turbines
and to some powerful God that made it all
and the sun too, from which every watt
measure of light comes, which is to say
my light switch is wired to eternity.

NO SOLICITATIONS ALLOWED

That year we met, I think
You really meant it, that part
About "no way" at first but then
My foot got in the door somehow
And caused quite a stir among us
Both, next a whole history happened.

There are some things so wonderfully
Mysterious that even mountains will
Not say them out loud, and they
Will simply stand there
In silence and in love
Madly with the sun and rain,
And moon.
Forever.

MR. BIG

So many things are bigger than we are.
Take fate for example. And I have not
even mentioned love or luck, the trickiest
pair of gigants that ever came to town.
So can you blame us for a little boasting
bravado and bluster? For making puzzles
only we can solve. Heroes that wear
our clothes, dreaming our big dreams.
Look how we sneak around to the
front of the parade, pretending to lead.

12 HABITS OF THE POETIC LEADER

Make surprise your strategic plan.
Take stuck in stride and keep on going.
Be right only when you must.
Accept failure as your teaching friend.
Take the long way home when needed.
Put things together that don't belong.
Know the shortest route is often curved.
Be grateful even when it's not possible.
Make your path where none exist.
Practice the art of a wild, fierce now.
Integrate your head, heart and hara (body).
Pickle yourself with the stories you choose.

ONLY INK AND PAPER

We humans were custom made for poetry.
Happily firing synapses they sizzle and snap,
as if joy were an island not so far from here.
And the metaphors that mend hurting hearts
of their deep and unspeakable grief and pain.
Making patterns real, turning now into a shrine
called everything. And though only made of ink
and paper, they arc and spark and burn true.
Ask God your toughest questions, then listen
for the faint echoes to return. The answer
you hear will always, always ... be a poem.

SIGNS

After Mom died a lot of things changed
around here. Dad became a gifted reader
of signs, each one forged from her to him
each one placed with care on his daily walks.

Diverse omens found lying on the ground
pregnant with a type of urging and purpose.
She would forgive him for things he felt
needed forgiving and she would tell him things too.

Once she left a penny, weathered deceptively
green by neglect and with that year she died.
At other times she would remind him to be good,
to eat well, to make long distance calls on holidays.

Through other improbable messengers like
old post cards, broken pieces of jewelry, even old
tools and lost gas caps, each had a portion of the story
to tell and tell again.

For years now he has walked that same path, daily
while the signs have ebbed and flowed with the attentive
muscle of his grieving, hunger will always
speed the plough.

THE "BIG DATA" ON YOU?

All those tiny bits of data. Every where,
the dots of you left by your clicking
custom crafted by your index fingers.

What do your dots say about you?
What do your dots say that you do
not know they say about you?

And exactly who is connecting them?
Who is saying, hmm, then yes or no?
And why are they saying either one?

Don't worry though, it is not your fault,
what you like or love is just you, that's all.
Big data knows everything like a prayer.

SUN TRAIL

Look. The poppies
they are at it again
exploding on the
hills with their deep
yellow flames and
supple hearts.

The tender green pines
the red manzanita
the wild iris, low and steady –
they all breathe the
secrets of the dark soil
from where the poppies came.

And they bend slightly to praise
the golden parachutes
who in turn pour themselves
joyfully, opening
without restraint up and
toward the sun.

As the black bellied poppies
teach with tender care
how to close up shop
daily, to forget what
needs forgetting.

How not to shrink
from these sanguine
spring hills
at the first sign of
happiness.

IT'S OK

In this town, the regular people
order plain black coffee and drive cars
that rarely turn heads
nor show up in off-road mountain scenes.

We stand on line at coffee shops
and are mostly quiet, just behind
large–calved, handsome men with special
bike shoes and beautiful women with bright

yellow-flamed spandex pants and
bikes that cost
more than
house rent for a year.

We listen patiently to overheard cell phone tips
we are unlikely to ever use and are amazed
at coffee drinks that require as many
as nine good words to order.

There is nothing wrong with
being rich or beautiful or both.
You can even drink double, non-fat, large,
extra foam, dry, decaf, lattes.

We don't mind.
It's ok.

ELEVEN QUESTIONS WE MIGHT ASK IN A QUIET MOMENT

1. Considering what we know of winter, do you suppose it could ever lose its way in this world, forgetting how to freeze?

2. Could we change the meaning of a drought by simply remembering what the cactus knows?

3. Why is it that the only attack that's nearly impossible to defend against, is the one that's unintended?

4. How much evil is created in this world by those whom are constantly fighting it?

5. Do you suppose God knew the butterfly and the humming bird would so rarely rest?

6. And does Jesus that sweet profit descend into hell like Dante, periodically bargaining for a few more souls?

7. Living inside the house of greed, doesn't fear seem like our best and most trusted friend?

8. If we could measure for example the amount of love inside a house, could we count that in the appraisal?

9. Do you suspect the crow with his bold head and beautiful wings considers black to be the color of sorrow?

10. Do you think that snakes ever pity us for living so far away from the sacred ground?

11. And what question is your life asking ... Oh, and did you do the choosing?

MIRACLES

When the smallness of my vision
Dampens all hope inside, I simply watch
And these clumsy feet keep moving.

When what could have been
Turns bitter and dusty from wear
I feel the tinniest move as a miracle.

When the bit is cold in my mouth and
When daylight reveals only a potholed
Road, just the sound of my feet can comfort.

Rising up from this pain is not grand or special
If it says anything it says star dust knows
It says come with me just one more time.

Miracles always have their own strange rhythm
To know them is to place power into the possible
And God as surprised as anyone when they happen.

EXECUTIVE PRESENCE

Oh how dearly we want it,
That illusive look, that just-right feel
That not to warm, not to cold stance
That calm, centered confidence
The gravitas that says I can.

Oh how dearly we want it,
To hide our sweating palms
To ease our speedboat heart
To say to the world, yes I matter
And later, to begin believing it too.

KEEPING TRACK OF MY COURAGE

I sometimes find you in the garden
staring at the tomatoes, contemplating
the weeds or maybe just gazing at

the sunflowers, amazed at the weight
those thin legs can bear. You can be
found indoors in winter slyly turning

down the thermostat. Often I worry when
you are gone. I ask, will you come back? And
will we even recognize one other if you do?

When you are close by I worry about
different things though certain noises
downstairs late at night are not as scary.

THIS IS DAYLIGHT

This is daylight and
it will make no excuses
for its speed dies quicker
in winter, watched or not.

It shows stories of calm and heat
and it's battles have been fought
everywhere we have defended.
So much that when great black

bears rise in spring laying out
their sweetest schemes of being.
Yes, that is a warmth so familiar,
Yes, that is a daylight so near.

WORDS

Every word is a prejudice.
– Nietzsche

These are brilliant words you speak.
Just saying them seems right, and
not even or because of their meaning.
Which only matters anyway as much
as the purr they make as the sound
rushes forward into each new purpose.

Listen, you can feel words, their roots
rising and the rain as its coming along
and down each tiny travailing path to
meet and bless these always growing
everywhere sounds of words singing.

Like some kind of music that asks why?
Like some kind of prayer that answers yes.
Without any sound. Without any word.
Up underneath, where the real meaning
lives and listens to how it all flows through.
Every word I tell you was once a dream.

WHO ARE YOU?

We usually answer such questions about
ourselves with some good, steady nouns.
I'm a son, a brother, a husband. a friend.
I am a poet, a coach, a martial artist.

But we are also verbs too, maybe
even more so as we get older and older
moving toward the flute end of our lives.
My yearned for verb is always inspiration!

As it dances daily with my stuck.
This life of mine is mostly a fine
and tame living built upon prose.
But also (sometimes) with a wild heart
shocked and astonished poem by poem.

A DOZEN THINGS THE PACK-MULE POET KNOWS:

1. Poetry isn't rarefied or highfalutin but made for the rest of us from sweat, joy and mud.

2. The best poetry begins in delight and ends in wisdom and never the other way around.

3. Great poems can be simple and complex, wakeful and exhilarating, confrontative and healing.

4. Poems are just stories without all the boring parts, words that have learned jujitsu.

5. Often poems aren't even fair, saying what they don't mean and doing what words alone can't do.

6. Great poetry traffics in saying what is real and true, having an intense allergy to baloney and BS.

7. You can't force a poem to do anything, but once it decides to do something you can't stop it either.

8. Poems are bifocals for the soul, news that stays news, words from which there is no retreat.

9. Great poems operate down deep in the soil and bramble of life, the rag and bone shop of the heart.

10. A poem is like the belly of a shark, able to digest it all: grief, joy, anger, fear, paradox – anything.

11. Every word is a prejudice, every simile a map, each metaphor a railroad track that leads somewhere.

12. The greatest poems have gifts for the head (ideas), for the heart (emotions) and for the hara (body).

GALILEO'S TELESCOPE

I tore myself away from the safe comfort of
certainties / Through my love for truth; and truth
rewarded me. – Simone de Beauvoir

He must have been just a little mad
the way his waking dreams made no sense
the way he loved light, the way
for years he lived inside the lion's mouth.
He was a heretic, of that we are certain, but
he did not want to die in darkness,
of course, and he pleaded with great skill
not for his own life, but for theirs.

He pleaded for them to simply look
through the long limb of his telescope into the
shapeless endlessness of their own heaven.
Therefore, he stood for a type of commonality
for small pieces of hard-earned wisdom.

What is true must be so, he would say
for what is true is always before us,
and we are already living it anyway.
They looked at him with harsh
thin faces, their golden eye glasses rising in the air
perched on the tips of their noses.
Often he would think of his friends
he would think of the lovers he had
ignored or forsaken. The displeasure of

so many around him, for this,
this single passion. This obsession
to know something of the secret.

To hold back that desperate thing come to
frighten him now into a new obedience
come to lure him from his bright dreams
to the safety of firm and steady ground.

THE MONK

There was this monk who flew
often and particularly through
New York and other such major cities.
Like any good monk he flew economy
and would often decline the peanuts
until everyone else had been served.
And then send his small black polished
begging bowl down the isle because of
course he would not disobey the seat belt
sign and also did not want to insist.

Over time having built up a great
reservoir of compassion for his
fellow travelers, he calculated how
many person years were wasted
each day taking our shoes on and off
in the security line. He prayed for
the freedom of abstract thinking
that one day we would realize the
power of metaphor and how the
law of analogy means the next
hiding place will not be our soles.

IN PRAISE OF THE UNCOMMON TOMATO PLANT

Don't fool yourself, or think things calm,
the tomato plant is no easy child to rear.
Unlike the mild and subdued potato, happy
with that slow and secluded darkness
the tomato plant rides the edges of my
planter box like some wild stranger.
She grows inches per hour
fills every space with her pungent persistence,
holds a thousand green questions at once,
refusing to ripen even one until she is ready,
until she has had her fill of heat, sweet soil, and water.
Early Girl, Beefsteak, names we use mean nothing
While her reckless body pours itself
down dry summer gullies, across fields
of wild blackberry
While her impossible red fruit grows more
dense and delicious by the day.

HUNTERS AND GATHERERS

A careless God leaves good lessons
lying around everywhere. Things that
could really help someone, but that are
obscured by too much time elapsed
between the action that bears the fruit
and the silence that bears the boredom.
Our job as hunters and gatherers is
to look for these things just lying around.
To try and make a few good stories out
of those pieces of abandoned wisdom.
God won't mind and it might help a little.

MY FRIEND HAPPINESS STEALS

Even now we're stealing precious time
from our to-do lists. Like bacteria in a
petri dish, those items never run out
of food or will for constant replication.

Now I am supposed to be sweeping
the house, throwing out the garbage
and doing god knows what else.

But instead I am writing this and
happily hidden away deep inside
my own fierce and wondering heart.

Now with my wayward and larcenist
friend who models a certain kind
of courage and stubborn rascality.
Happiness, the one who steals.

YOUR TO DO LIST IS YOUR ENEMY

Forget responsibility, commitment!
Your to do list is your enemy now
or at least the friend of your enemy.
Next time run, hide, obfuscate, do
what it takes to get free. No really,

that list is like a tar baby to you,
notice how you never get loose.
It eats a thousand check marks
for just one snack and twice
that many for even a light meal.

Finish it all, smile then bask in your
goodness, a complete contented soul.
No. It's a trap. It will never happen.
Best to dodge, weave and ignore -
go to your grave with your Visa

unpaid, light bulbs unchanged.
I tell you its better to sing that one
sweet song, that one little poem.
Let God make your check marks,
the only ones that ever counted.

REPORT TO THE EXECUTIVE COMMITTEE

Suddenly every word you say
you measure first, carefully
held on your tongue for some
wiser part of the brain
to perform a kind of
safety control check. A
million years of evolution goes
into each filtered sound you make.

Now. One false move
and you like the salmon
will take your last
death flight, writhing
in the iron claw of the eagle and
you thought we were only
discussing the inventory overages, how
the sales figures are a little off.

ADVICE FOR BLOODHOUND WRITERS: COHERE ...

Tiny nudges,
everywhere.
Hunches from
others,
the news and
your muse,
mistakes, typos.

Follow them all,
sprawl with them.
Sniff down trails.
Your nose won't lie.
Listen to me. Really,
you can't help
but find what's there.

PREPARATIONS

For Jaime, Don, and Mike

All that is left me now
      for the doing, is a kind
of slow persistence. A practice?

Trusting the body is hard work, the small flaring voice, the big
feelings, the frantic calls we send out across the lakes' balmy
surface, trusting that one day, in their own time, the answers will
come.

The gifts I must give in this world,
      I must give.

One day
soon enough I will disappear
into that mirror, as we all must.
      Without trying, without struggle it is hoped.
Just as we had always dreamed.

Then, the mystery will become
my house once again, and all
the old secrets will live there too.

      Death a moment, just
like this one.

SELF IMPROVEMENT

At one time
in my life
I felt as though
I were finished, all

washed up,
done for,
a complete
and utter failure.

Now, I am
merely lost at
sea, wandering aimless
and confused.

It's a little better,
don't you think?

GOD'S "STATE OF THE CREATION" ADDRESS

Like Nietzsche, I know many of you
are waiting for a new religion to evolve, to be invented
or discovered or simply refashioned from all the
others that are used, but just barely. It's fine but I'm
not sure that's the point.

I mean how many times do I need to visit this place?
In your dreams you have imagined someone more
contemporary perhaps, more like Captain Kirk than
Moses, and that's OK. Really, I don't care.

But let me put it this way, I'm not scheduled back to
this place any time soon. You're on your own now with
all the wisdom the muse's have already served up.

After all, how many ways do I need to say that part
about – *"Do unto others ..."*
And what about the other thing you've hardly
ever been able to pull off – *"Love your enemies."*

And here is one last thing. I want you to forget about
that judgment day business. I'm not bringing anything
like that around here: no brim stones, no hell fire and
certainly no damnation, I don't do damnation.

BUDDHA'S LIPS

I don't know how you
do it, sitting there
for centuries
legs crossed
so quiet, like stone
　　　which after all

you are
but then again meditation
is a church too, A feeling.
A day without all those normal
threats: work, family, to do list.

No one knows, after all
　　　where dreams actually
come from, a soul, maybe summer?
I know this. Whatever it is
that makes your stone lips smile
　　　that's for me.

WINTER RAIN STORM

All night we watched
the eucalyptus trees bow this way
then that nearly exhausted trying to
please the wind. So many demands!

Living close to land's edge is not easy.
The ocean is anything but charming and its
wildness reminds us how the wind
is only one of its many faces.

Now that this winter
storm, its scattered limbs and torn leaves,
has lodged itself
just outside our door.

We can pray for rain in earnest.
Pray always for what has already
happened, for how the world
is glancing back in your direction.

And God's love will more easily find you.

MULTI-LEVEL MARKETING

At a potluck party someone leans toward you slowly,
brie and cracker in one hand, Chardonnay in the other
and asks if you know about the new supplements, the
ones that make your bladder last for ever. That's when
you begin to realize that staying young and having
longer periods between bathroom visits really matters.
And after all a well functioning waste removal system
may just be your passport to happiness.

It seems they are planning a small gathering next
Thursday evening to which you are now invited to
discuss the amazing opportunity for new health and
financial freedom as well, absolutely no pressure
(if you know what I mean).

Suddenly you feel your feet become restless, your toes
twitching for the door just below the black, shinning
leather that contains them. You barely have time to blurt
out how you must excuse yourself for the bathroom,
where those soft azure towels wait and the sandalwood
scented candles quietly burn.

> "Here is my business card" you hear
> faintly in one ear as you take your bladder and
> leave.

A ROOM

Somewhere there is a large room that
holds everything that has not happened
that waits just before for thin possibilities.

The delicate sounds of all this unmade history
can be barely heard above the din of all our troubled
predictions. A crowd of witnesses looks out a window
searching the horizon for some clear sign but
everything for them keeps coming back with that
dull and familiar tonality.

A few others, outcastes that barely belong here,
have gone inside themselves for their prophecies
but can only chant around the roughest edges of
what they have found there.

You who come years from now will inherit this room,
although we pray its walls will by then feel like air. Here,
I give you a window, a way of speaking, a few bare words
and the same brilliant mystery that for a moment was mine.

NIGHT SONG

For Judy

There is no quiet like a winter night,
where The Great Horned Owl waits at land's
edge in total stillness seeing all that is there
with those enormous yellow eyes set in that broad face,
each wing specially designed to deliver a fierce talon
razor–like through the undisturbed air.

Look at the window, it is snowing there
hard through the darkness and the old stars
wait too. They tremble against a cold wind,
that breathes constantly down upon this world
and everything in it.

Can we learn inside the still darkness
of the night our true history,
learn to praise the deep story
of all we might become tonight? Our legend.
This world's undeniable beauty: its green,
furred, feathered, or flippered things!
This world's unbearable sadness too.
        What else did we expect?
Now let us pray together.
Now let us sing each other home.

JESUS AND THE FOCUS GROUPS

When Jesus openly ignored the corporate culture and
the organizational chart too, and sent out that memo
ordering up the first few focus groups we knew we
were all headed for a kind of deep trouble.

It was budget review time and even the calmest
disciples were tense. On the day of the focus groups
Jesus led them himself and they went just fine so long
as he served up that home—made wine and besides
who throws stones around two-way mirrors?

He brought the house down with that golden rule idea,
I mean who could argue?
But then the part came out about the meek and the
poor, about rich people trying to pass camels through
eyes of needles and half the crowd walked out fearing
higher taxes.

When he barely whispered the part about loving our
enemies and turning the other cheek, you could have
heard a pin drop. "I don't think they are buying it,' said
the VP of Marketing slouching toward the door,

but Jesus he just kept smiling, just kept pouring the
wine saying those impossible things, like he actually
thought we could pull it all off.

FRIENDS LEAVING

(For Marv and Kay)

I look out a friend's living room
Window to see the ancient world
The ten thousand things busily
Being themselves: birds, leaves,
Sky, grass, sounds, trees, blue.
And then there is the real estate
For sale sign, different time, fast
Time going like they are going
Far away. Friends leaving.
Many kinds of time. Wind time
Rock time. sad time,
Friends leaving.

ON BEING CASUALLY ASKED THE QUESTION:
HOW ARE YOU DOING?

Well I've answered
that question many
times, of course, and
I do the best I can to stay
fresh, alert and honest
in my responses,
engaged fully at times
even though its
usually asked in passing
and in mostly old and
rather tired ways.

Actually my answer
often seems to
me more than a little
sparse at times, nearly
weightless in fact, much
like a famished,
green-helmeted
hummingbird,
I too, often live that
kind of frenetic life
changing from one
flower to the next
so quickly.

You see when it comes
right down to it, I am
always "many ways"!
And when I really
think about it and even
when I am very sure that
you really do want
to know my answer,
I am never sure
which part of me
you are asking.

IF I WERE LIKE WILLIAM STAFFORD

If I were like William Stafford
I would study that thin river that points
to the ocean, and the hills too just beyond my window.
Like a hawk with deep lantern eyes
I'd live inside the stillness of winter
no motion would be wasted either,
pulling up occasionally, even faltering
at times on the frayed edge of the wind, looking down,
always looking down and nothing
would ever be missed or ignored.

If I were like William Stafford
I would live as simply as yellow headed
weeds live on the distant edge of a garden
growing strong on drops of water
and a fraction of the light that a tamed rose needs.
I would love things for their invisible fullness
and because they did not yet have shape
I would gently reach inside feeling about
for some faint meaning until
the sun would rise.

I would build many a place
that no road could ever reach or disturb
seed gardens of deep silence
that others might taste a harvest,
a new and sweet crop from their own planting.

If I were like William Stafford, I would never
stray far from the wisdom of wild water
those streams of darkness
and how the river listens that
is how I would listen.

DEMOCRACY

*The Constitution and Bill of Rights are designed to mitigate a basic truth:
"No one is going to do the right thing all the time. But whatever you say
about America, it's still intrinsically capable of correcting itself. . ."*
– Jacob Needleman

Now, as in every other moment before
this one, our democracy remains as fragile

and elusive as common happiness. A present danger
always rising, "the last best hope for human kind"

said Lincoln, and one easily imagines he
meant what he said

on that battlefield made sacred by canon and blood.
Stranger things have held a people together. Love

as glue is mighty but so tenuous and difficult too.
Fear and greed are tiresome, but a potent pairing,

each of these twins makes powerful kindling.
A brilliant blaze which never lasts.

"Democracy," I tell you, "is no thing at all."
It is the invisible current of a dark and raging river.

It is all vision, all paradox, derived of stillness and movement,
it is amazing alchemy to the very bone.

THE HAWK IS LIKE THE HEART

*"The antidote to weariness is not necessarily
rest but rather it is wholeheartedness."* – Brother David

The hawk is like the heart,
both on a glorious, difficult journey.
Soaring high, riding great waves of wind.

Fierce and free and true,
cleaved forever to a great desire,
to the winged ecstasy of delight.

But just as cold and storm can stall
a great bird's flight, so to can sadness
and loss turn the heart away from itself.

A bone-tired weariness in need of tending,
with those healing, fierce and awakening words.
For such labor is the soul's most sacred work

and such labor is all our most sacred work.
So let the heart be fed at it's healing altar
for it must not fail, and it can not falter.

HOME

One day, you will look west. Out toward that far
horizon, and there you will find a deep, silent
river. Even now, it waits for you, knows your name.
It lies just beyond where all our times begin, just
beyond that stand of live oaks you see each
morning through your window after waking.

Its currents are fast and true, and receives all
that flows there from some greater source that
even the sun cannot easily find. Maybe you have
seen that river in your dreams and maybe you

know how its mud red banks
fill with a chorus of wild poppies and lilacs
each spring, how the willows along both
sides kneel down to pray in winter.

You suspect that river will spell out
one day the words that mean how you
and the others came to be here.
And will someday show you,
your long path home.

COYOTE MEDITATION

We have always lived close by,
yet in our own world. After all,
our fur and four legs, are thicker
and faster than yours.
Night time without lights?
We can still see to hunt.

Like you, we eat and mate
in every season,
and though you wonder deeply
as to the meaning of our
wild gardens,
we plant nothing, yet harvest it all

you see, it never occurred to ever leave Eden,
in the first place, we and haven still constant friends
and so the specter of death doesn't haunt our howling,
or turn our warm dens into houses of dread,
which is to say, and as far as coyotes go,
we keep on singing, right up till the end.

HOPE

In an old iron pot, food cooks just fine:
slow, juicy, and delicious,
where greens and garlic,
celery and cayenne meld themselves
into some scrumptious new dish.

Hope is that way too,
it mixes well with a little observation,
just a dash of advice, along with something
someone we once loved dearly said
when we were young and afraid.

Often a big heaping portion of
the way we want it to be,
gets added at the last minute,
until the taste grows and grows
so much sweeter than true.

CALLING DAD

For the third time
this week you told me
that the reception
was not good and lightly
accused me of intentional
cell phone interference.
But tonight striding care-
fully thru darkness I held
the telephone high
above my head as
if to help it drink in
those digital words
you kept on sending.

Complaints really about
the stairs, the food, the rain
and how last week your cable
television kept going out
as you adjusted buttons
you no longer understand.
And as you flailed out at
other changes you never
requested, as you hung on
out of breath and out of
tricks and treats and tethers,
clutching hard to a long held life,
now deep into the narrows.

ARE YOU A LEADER?

As soon as we start
throwing the word leader
around we get in trouble.
We start thinking
it is simply a noun.
We start thinking that
having the title
means something.

Leadership is a verb.
Anyone can lead.
Often people in leadership
positions are the last to lead.
It means we take
risks by saying what
needs to be said and done, not
simply what's wanted or expected.

Think Martin Luther King, Jr.,
Think Abraham Lincoln,
Think Sojourner Truth.
They were not always
courageous, no one is.
They did not always
lead, no one does,
but often they did.

DEMAGOGUERY

It is not easy
to lead even
in this way. It
takes energy
and intelligence
to play on fear.
To incite hate.
To help others
be unresponsible.
To snarl: "It's them!"
No, it's not easy to do,
and did I mention how
it destroys the heart
of the demagogue
and the demagogued too.

LET US USE POETRY

Let us use poetry
to slow down
just a little
to let our souls
catch up with
the rest of us
so that then we
can remember
who we actually are
so that then we can
finally grieve more fully
celebrate with abandon
laugh and cry and laugh
again. Let us use poetry
to sing our selves home.

SHAME PRAYER

Dear Lord, let me have just the right amount of guilt
for it is a potent corrective which goes a long way.
Let me see and feel what makes this world
more real and right. Let me hear my own internal
voices, the ones best suited for the job at hand.
Like a useful storm let me hear as well my critical voice,
though like guilt, it will also work best in moderation.
Oh Lord, let even shame show its face now and again
for a small measure of fear can sometimes protect.
But help me remember to always keep fear slightly
off guard, somehow at bay by faith which doesn't falter.
But whatever you do God please do not let shame
set up shop in that extra room I have up stairs.
For shame has long been known to covet that space,
that very room you and I will so desperately need
one day for making my best dreams come true.

THE FULL HEART

Moderation is about
avoiding extremes.
Greed is about seeking them.

The heart prefers
another neighborhood
all together.

IN THE KINGDOM OF STRANGERS

In the kingdom of strangers,
how do we live out our lives
within those small tight spaces
of loneliness always signaling?

For without the kindnesses of
those we do not know but
whom let us walk step by step,
there beside their breathing.

More intimate than we pretend,
thrust into a place where time
does not harm or even want to.
For it's there that we must be

as strangers, but cleaved together
full, fast and forever into the one.
No stranger at all, but tested by our
connection, saved by our particular.

THE GRATEFUL WAY

It is more mole-like than you might think.
A practice, a habit, a response to any old miracle
that happens by. It burrows deep into the earth
and then just waits. Yes, ailments and complaints
they have their ways too, moving swiftly through
weary hearts by the fuel of a common practice.
But to live in the earth, deep down where
hidden veins of gold begin their shinning;
That is God's grateful way—and surely it abides.

THE STORM

The switch grass leans this way and that
rioting in the fields near the roadside,
blown red and reckless by the wild winds.
A low ceiling of dark clouds obscures what little
courage I once had.

Goose bumps form where any minute
lightening could strike. While the animal that
is inside me hides and cowers in timeless fear.
Like a tree I make my final stand, right
here leafless and bare.

Ripped open by the cold fierce winds and
their icy shards of regret. Branches laid bare
and broken by the weight of sleet and snow.
A frigid feeling no warmth of winter
sun could ever touch.

But I have also known the sweet sublime
caresses of summer, from some place
deep, the sap rising just to say I am here.
While all along, my roots lit on fire by
love's lightening touch.

HOW A GRUDGE GROWS

No one knows how it starts.
Some small slight or rolled
eye during a critical negotiation,
just one "that's ridiculous" uttered
at precisely the right time, spoken
in anger or irritation or both
is usually all that's necessary.

Take the crow for example,
how he sits like a machine for
hours making bitter sounds,
blaming the world even
for the things he loves,
or the dog that's tied up
in some back yard that

by habit, barks and howls
night after night.
Like these
stones flung
from my hand,
then yours,
again and again.

VOICE LESSONS

You, and all the others
have so many voices
inside. Each one
vying for attention.
The voice of doubt, yes
and that of fear, always.
The voice of wisdom,
There too but faint.
A voice of memory
that warns, guides.
And the voice of courage,
that quivers, but holds still
all the other voices.
And then,
says it any way.

YES

We think the view from somewhere else will be better,

that the raging river will get slower, the desert less dry.

We think there will finally be time for everything,

especially for calmness, quiet and living by earth-time.

We think to our selves: *stop the world, I want to get on,*

but the world is just too merciful for that.

It keeps calling out to us *YES,* again and again,

let's not get caught constantly whispering *NO.*

MIA

In a war
like Vietnam
thirty plus years later
many bodies still
absent
missing in action
with entire lives
dedicated to
finding the long
white bones
of loved ones
hoping that some small
piece of a dream
might still be
attached.

SEEDS

How do they know? a friend once asked me. Know what?
I said. To not send their tender roots skyward, to not
have their tiny tentacles left dangling in the drying sun.

And to not send those beautiful leaves and flowers helplessly
downward into a soil that couldn't care less."You ask strange
questions," I said, trying to pretend that I wasn't amazed.

Seriously, he said. "You can throw those seeds into the ground
any way you want, and they somehow know exactly what to do."
OK, I said. "It's called gravitropism." "The ability of plants to sense

and alter their growth in response to gravity." That's when he
looked at me and just smiled. "Naming is easy," he said. "They don't
have a clue do they?" Then I smiled and said, "no they really don't."

I AM CONFIDENT

I am confident.
It rhymes with I am ready.
It is the feeling we most need.

It is the opposite of I am stressed.
It's faithful companion is I am still afraid,
but willing to step into the breach anyway:

into the chasm, the gap between where we
are and where one fine day surely we must be.

JUST FOR YOU

Someone much wiser than me.
No wait, let me start over again.
Somewhere inside me there
is a place of struggle and grace.
That place lives by the power of faith and naming.
It turns and corrects itself by a kind of stumbling.
Wading upon the waters of not quite knowing,
that flow only when the salmon are far at sea.
How can we keep spring's explosions
from burning our whole house down?
With its constant radiances and revelations.
How can we sing without proper words
Or rhythm or even a foot to tap to the music?
I know these questions have no easy answers,
why do you think I gave them to you?

REMEMBERING OUR TOGETHER

Just yesterday some new memory
came to light and to live inside me.
Like a magnet, it pulled from the future.
Sprawling sounds suddenly everywhere.
It said "hey, do that again and again,"
which was the whole idea I think.
It was God whispering her pure wisdom.
It was a shuddering of our whole story,
this earth determined to round us true.
Suddenly stars leaned in toward one another
and forward like this into our best dreams.
But finally it was your loving gaze that did it all.
Some hot white light showing me everything
all at once, and then love . . . just a little more.

ANY AFTERNOON

Any afternoon can become
itself or some other thing if it wishes
can grow light and airy
wear the clothing of joy or surprise
can soothe, or pleasure in some way.
Or bear down upon us

heavily, of course, like a
steel claw, like a vise
like hearing about
a young boy whose body
has suddenly formed into a
dark pocket filling with cancer.

I heard the doctor say
to that boy that his hurting, hairless
body could stand no more radiation
no more chemicals
no more treatment at all.
"Now" said the Doctor

"Its in God's hands"
and I wondered
to myself –
who's hands
had it been in
before?

THE TRICKSTER POEM

It never enters directly thru the front door
and don't even think about receiving a call
to announce that its here, near or coming.

It is always the "not quite what you thought"
surprise that does the work worth doing,
that nails you so firmly to your-new-you.

It points out across the field and shouts,
hey look over there, what's that moving?
All the while some fierce beast is

sneaking back behind you, firm
on all fours barely touching your
unsuspecting calves and then the

poem whispers something so delightful,
so stunning, so not what you expected
which in effect means ... push then tumble.

GRIEF

And what about grief? Notice
how it learns the contours of our bodies
soft and hidden

places, such an unwelcome
visitor we say, what purpose
might you

have? Invading the
slow, barely functioning
mind

like a thin blade
like a free
fall off some

crumbling cliffs edge
the soul tending to the
soul, its own

broken self. Or, did you
think grief only a symptom,
a sickness

to be cured?

DEAR EVERY ONE:

What say we wean ourselves from this desperate habit of predicting happiness? And for good too. After all our best songs come unbidden, shrouded in mystery. And those places we thought were the happiest aren't even places at all. It's only what's inside. Oceans of delight forming up patterns where least expected, just like those tidal waves of despair. Oh yes, they happen too. It is only the cradle of your mind that shows your best most lovely house. And its only real name is . . . well Wakeup! Please let us hear from you. I mean aren't you just a little surprised . . . that there is anything here at all!

Sincerely yours,
The Universe

COMPLAINTS

Like crows they have learned to live everywhere.
In every part of the day or country it seems.
Sure, they like rain or clouds, but
even sunshine has a few hidden inside.

Whole towns have created celebrations in their honor
and name themselves by such tales of hard times and woe.
If two strangers meet the most natural way to
befriend one another is by exchanging them.

As in "Think the sun will ever come out again?"
Or "what about those taxes?"
And complaints have their whole history too
even in God's house – how heaven itself

was just one long reaction to hell.
And how we talked about, even there
the harps out of tune, that old useless choir
and how it droned on and on.

Oh the burden
of such a difficult paradise,
this hard-time eternity
that never ends.

BETTER THAN GOD

We must each feel the whole earth now, shaping our names
with it's teeth and hands, it will tell what we need to know
spelling out our secret music with a fiery circle of tapping feet
and the claiming of that far-off horizon with our eyes.

We must make our arms stronger and stronger
while giving up all traces of anger and bitterness.
We must fill our mouths with better memories
and with better words than darkness alone can say.

We must burn with new faith, glisten with rightness
we must dive inside ideas that are good and true and just,
each promising to embrace the real.
We must promise to sing the world right again,

and for heaven's sake
its arc rising there
toward some invisible place,
even better than God.

GRATEFULNESS

Each day the engine of my gratefulness
must be coaxed and primed into action.
Of course like any old clunker,
it would just as soon stay put.
For even after the labored start beats the inertia,
and the plume of white smoke struggles upward,
the same hills always appear,
soaring daily – tall and ominous as before.

There is the long slow hill of "aging"
so gradual and smooth at first.
And then that steep grade called "the news."
Yes, and always some mountain of a war
looming out there, never too far in the distance.

Even an old idea or a feeling long abandoned
might conspire to halt this fragile progress –
valves sputtering, tires flattening, clutch slipping.
But the old "potato, potato, potato" sound
of the engine, and all its mysterious fuel,
for which I am truly grateful
somehow
keeps stumbling along.

THE FEELING COMES FIRST

Having lived inside a body
for all these years. I know
something about waiting.

I have read carefully
the instruction manuals for
living in this mysterious form.

Still their words lay flat
as time creeps forward, while
only the easy things get done.

Motivation is always a strange
land that the heart can never
find without some real longing.

The hard stuff we accomplish
I mean the really hard things
forever bind to our new names.

The hard stuff that requires a fall
so far that dying ourselves new
again is the only thing that works.

But none of it seems to happen.
No! Change that: it will not happen!
Until the feeling comes first.

MEMORIES
(On the five-year anniversary of James's Death)

All memories are horizontal
unless, of course, they are vertical.
They spread like fog across
any surface of differing temperatures.
When we feel them deeply,
they become fruit from the soul.
They live only for spring.
They hibernate with clouds.
They move easily with any storm.
They sing back your name,
even before it was yours.
They heal and hurt alike.
They peel from us even the thinnest
ways in which we hide or cover our hearts.
They make our making real.

I THOUGHT I WAS THE ONLY ONE

One mentor said when people pray
I have no idea what they are doing.
I nod and feel an odd kindred twinge.

Another says, I keep busy because
when not my antennae picks up strange
stations. I smile because my dial is
slanted and gravity takes me there too.

Some brave editorialist wrote of
depression and wanting no gun
in the house. I whisper shy agree-
ment, so low no one hears but me.

And just last week this poem I read said,
"at this ripe age I am more scared, jealous
and unsure of what I know than ever before."
I tell you this, I purred when I heard that.

NOTE TO REALITY

Exactly what are you saying
to me and the others here?
Dream big. And bold. Or step
carefully like this along the path.

No seriously, I want to know
how my feet should go
how my arms might open
just a little bit wider. For

playing it safe seems a strategy
that oceans, mountains, trees
and especially god
rarely employs.

A ZEAL FOR RESISTANCE

Never underestimate your opponent
nor the strange rules of paradox either.
Think gravity, water, wind, how the
world holds us near like a cloud
holds water, its constant changing.

Be the wild eyed lover living free
speak the words that will not allow
your retreat, be like a Dog Soldier
tie your bright red sash to a stake
in the fierce earth.

Declare your defiance
Declare your strange
love for resistance too,
for God only knows
what you can do then.

WHAT IS AT STAKE?

As we move through our lives
dancing some grand mystery
we ask, are some harvests
more critical than others? Yes.

Will there be more? Yes.

But can a dozen minor ones,
beautiful, bountiful, but smaller
make up for the one critical
harvest we missed? No.

UNHAPPINESS IS SO COSTLY

Unhappiness is such a costly habit
You feel that no one understands
So you keep on piling up evidence
Spending all those "no's" & "nots"
Punctuated by that occasional "Oh
My God" just to let us know you're
Serious about how much you'll invest.
In winter you growl its just too cold
In summer the humidity makes you ill
The clerk was nice but not so sincere
And the election did not go your way
The gas bill is high because of ...
Well we don't know why, that's the problem
All this precious treasure spent on grousing
All this sweet life just walking out the door.

COULD THIS GOLDFISH HELP YOU GET LOVED?

I am not kidding this was the title
of a morning message in my email.
It was the subject line too.
Of what? Should I call it spam?
After all help not asked for is

the whole purpose of poetry.
You start out the poem, reading it
or amazingly and especially writing it,
not knowing what is needed or
where the poem is taking you.

To surprise or shock or teach or heal?
And then by poem's end the rug that
you secretly wanted pulled right out from
under you, is pulled. And that self-loathing
fearful part that you so desperately hide

or even that false version of yourself
that you know is not real. It's all gone.
Cause instantly you "see" the world fresh
again. Yes this is you, that abiding
habit of yours, feeling each day that

something wild and new must be learned
which is the moment you turn to a tree or
to a beautiful bird or to a god knows what?
Maybe even to a kind and benevolent
goldfish who just may help you get loved.

WHY AM I HAPPY?

There is an easy answer for this.
The wind brings it along for the ride,
even when I can't hear what it says.

But still it tells of secret places and
rivers only the quiet can find, and
it knows what "given" really means.

Last night as I emptied the trash,
the moon lay so close in the sky
that I could barely open the lid.

And when I did get it open, even the
garbage seemed wise, while hungry
raccoons lay quiet in the bushes.

TODAY WE ARE ALL EXHAUSTED

Today we are all exhausted.
Our best dreams tired and deflated.
Like the old asters they barely breathe
in their beds. Even the dog is indifferent,
wagging his tail only slightly as we arrive.
As for our career – don't even ask.
Our money so carefully saved
has gone sadly missing.
And all our equity now belongs to another.
The poem penned with such excitement,
now sits listless next to the bed.
Seems even our bad ideas
have stopped coming for a while.

But then slowly you look away
Glimpsing far through the dust and darkness,
dismissing plans that never happened anyway.
Next, a little breeze comes through the window.
Then a beautiful bubble forms in your soup.
And the foam on the top of your coffee
begins to look a lot like Mt. Everest.
You feel that somewhere in the distance
There is just a schosh of music and laughter.
You can't quite hear or sing it yet,
but still your stubborn heart begins
tapping out that crazy little tune,
that no one else knows but you.

FEELING JUST RIGHT

Some day we may wake up so hard
that the trees turn into pillars of light
and even the ineffable flight of dead stars
will make us vibrate madly with desire.

Some day our feet may lift off with longing
And won't stop moving until a miracle happens
with land and ocean joined in delight
as the blue-green waves cover everything.

Some day even the weak will rise
shuffling off with the powerful
making up some new religion
they will whisper forgiveness
and then see what happens.

Some day everything will come alive
we'll see and feel the world new again
just as it is – a fresh story
rising and God finally getting a little rest.

Some day our dream will match a far-off perfection
the song and the words will get lucky and real
finding just where they want to be
for example: Sunlight, Music, Feeling just right.

SPEEDING UP THE INEVITABLE

The I don't need to change stance
is the fastest way to get there.

Just be the change instead
of talking so much about it.

Don't worry, when you see your
feet moving like this, you will know.

When you glance ahead
and the way looks just right.

When the doing gets juicy
just the doing I mean, then

your wings will have only
their one best song to sing.

DISTRACTION

The outer world, it knows how.
It rings door bells and shouts
out loud alarms from cars we wish
someone would just steal already.
It blows dirt and grit and leaves
after the lawn is cut with a gusto
and the kind of noise that would
disturb the dead and departed.

But by far, the worst distractions
come from a surprising place. The
nay-sayer, the big ugly gremlin, that
who-do-you-think-you-are whisperer.
That *too-big-for-your-pants* reminder.
That critic that eats when you eat
that sleeps when you sleep. The
one who lives down deep inside.

LEARNING HOW TO LOSE

You never know when winning could backfire.
For birds and other critters it happens all the time.
Say for example you could cross vast oceans or
deserts with a single push off any steady ledge.
But say you found yourself on some wrong continent.
Confused and slipping off the edge of lost rocks.
Somehow on the wrong island or in the wrong time zone.
What would you do having won the epic battle of gravity,
only to have the entire universe whisper, "whoops"!

DECIDING NOT TO WIN

One day you may decide not to win.
You might even say this but not mean it,
at least in the sense of losing a real fight,
or a battle or even your keys or phone.

I'm talking more about losing to now.
Loosing to this moment by moment sprawl,
this passing of time that eludes us all.
Oh you might catch a full second here
or there, but keeping things totally present

year after year is something only god can do.

I DO NOT WANT TO BE A GOOD LEADER

(Based upon a true story ... seen many times!)

The leader must decide daily
to say yes to this, no to that.
Feeling their way inside the thing
without destroying the thing.
To resolve the tension of paradox, so
often needed before the deed is done.

Because wisdom is not so easy,
nor is it cut or dry or fixed in time
by the mind's incessant sound-bites.
The obsessive need for naming it all,
for the internal critic's chattering claims
made upon each piece of our paradise.

I do not want to be a good leader,
I want to be an inevitable leader,
given what I know and who I am.
I want to lead from the same place
that I have learned and loved from.
I want to lead from my heart.

11 REASONS TO ENJOY THE JOURNEY

There never was a mountaintop that could
hold a candle to the long grateful walk up.

The sun sets on its own time and you never
quite know when that time will occur.

The purpose of dancing is not to get to
the other side of the room.

Progress is an idea that is so tantalizing
that it flips over into nonsense in a flash.

Every thing is really beginnings and endings
dressed up and masquerading as middles.

Art itself is the best advertisement for holding
sacred the journey as is breathing and sex.

Weed whacking is the only exception to
these rules but only if your back is sore.

It is hard to be desperately poor and
still be happy but it seems to happen.

It is even more hard to be desperately rich
and remain happy, but I think it's possible too.

I saw a dog yesterday who was old and
blind and peeing on the sidewalk, happily.

How many times have you thought something
would make you happy but didn't. I rest my case.

IT GETS LATE SO EARLY NOW

Yesterday was the 100th year anniversary
Of the first oil well dug by hand. Strange
How that meteor that killed the dinosaurs
Is now about to get us too. Listen, do you
Know that feeling you get while running
Down a long flight of stairs and not
Having to think much about each step, but
Going down quickly on body knowledge?

This is how we must know each other
And the streams and rivers that flow
Right out side the windows and doors
That we look out upon but so rarely see.
Scientist say we have likely passed a
threshold: The ability to do anything
meaningful about the changing climate.

The earth's slow scream that we re-
fuse to hear or see or feel. The thing
is this: evil isn't local any longer.

COMPOST

I invite the color of darkness to rise
up and speak clearly on behalf of all
that's leaving this edge of the world.

In one form only to come back
as another. Like those limp carrots
kept too long in the plastic crisper.

Or the partially eaten salad from last
week and the avocado skins dropped
fruitless into our silver pail of compost.

All manner of bugs made happy
in that big pile of almost gone, while
the tomato plants rise in anticipation.

The sun feeling its way across hill after
hill, celebrating all the nearly departed
forms and those sacred ways of dying

and growing. The Christ-like
resurrection that is my garden
each and every magical year.

A POEM IS A CAT

A poem is a cat.
A dog is prose.
A cat sniffs,
circles around
stealth-like then
comes or doesn't.
A dog barks, wags
his tail and goes
where you command.
Like prose dogs follow
straight lines where
point A is the dog and
point B is the food.
A dog is lovable, yes
and does as told.
A cat is lovable, yes
but never does.

ATOMS ARE CRAZY

Atoms are crazy. Maybe more so
than any other stuff we've come
to know and love and kind of understand.
See, there are things smaller and bigger
than we will ever know or measure.
And it still makes us nervous when light
won't decide: Am I a wave or a particle?

Still all this had a strange kind of relative
feel and God was not granting interviews
to clarify until shortly before Einstein died.
God said, I will never play dice with this
universe, at least according to Einstein.
For me though, I'm not so sure. How do you
think the Atoms learned the best 2 out of 3?

PALOMA

Our cat
that sleek
and sensuous
caramel–colored muscle.
Pours herself effortlessly
through the kitchen
over the hardwood
of the entry–way
into the bath.
Not to take one.
But to ledge–walk
close by
the bubbles she loves,
close by the excited danger
of wet fur.

OF COURSE

This slightly "off" feeling,
like something important
has been forgotten, like
someone is about to deliver
wonderful news, or
maybe terrible news.
As if some long worried
event will never happen
or will always happen.
As if only I could
get back far enough
to see that long arc
of history that Martin
described. As if only
I could purchase some
thing good with all the
attention I have paid.
As if Jesus or the Buddha
could reach across and
just smile at me.
And say of my life . . .
Of course, my friend
Of course.

FOLLOW YOUR OWN WEIRD

Every poem is an invitation to strange.
To looking at life just a little askance.
Of seeing the old as new, the standard
as miraculous, the tattered old hat
as a new chapeau.

THE MORAL DILEMMA OF YELLOW

Who decided on the color of traffic signals?
I'll admit that red is an exciting color,
and it does do strange things to our
nervous system. Perhaps it was always
destined to be the color of – don't go.
But what of green?
Why not blue or hot pink or turquoise even?
All these colors, it seems to me,
are perfectly capable of signaling the brain
to press down upon the gas pedal. But then
comes the most troubling question of all.
Why should yellow have been given the
entire burden of yield? Of slowly doing
less on purpose. Of not taking it all.
Of exercising even a modest restraint,
of asking that most irreverent and holly
question of all – how much is enough?

REFRAME

Reframe is a verb and so are we. It is

the one word every person must carry

inside her or him for them and beyond.

Little do we know when hard feelings

come that we will need to abandon

that tired old habit of self loathing.

Listen, I'm not trying to say yin

can somehow be divorced from yang.

And I'm certainly not trying to improve

the way water always finds its easiest path.

The thing is this, there are no things really.

Nouns are just verbs playing dangerous.

GLOBAL WARMING

If you think earth is going to speak up
to tell us precisely what is happening
you would be wrong for three reasons.

One: Earth only hums now and then
And the language is too low to hear.

Two: Earth used to speak every language
But it sounded a lot like ocean waves storming.

Three: Earth loves silence as much as
sound and so we may not be favored.

POEM FOR THE UNDERDOGS

"Kill the Indian, and Save the Man"
– Capt. Richard C. Pratt

Here is some history worth the telling and telling again
of each necessary betrayal, of each of your required defeats.
Still we have named countless cities and towns and parks
too after all the places you once lauded or lived,
or hunted or fished or gathered anything that was left.

One day perhaps, many years from now we may
even formulate some new kind of belief or religion,
after the particular way your early people perished.
But, of course, that is not a promise you understand,
for you are still the underdogs, and we are still the over.

GETTING CLEAR

When "woe is me"
turns to "yeah for me"

When "I can't have it" shifts,
to look how powerful I am when

I choose not to. Look! The
picture just got a little clearer.

Didn't it.

THE DAYS OF YOU

You pour your big heart into everything,
your family and friends are lucky and loved.

But what about those days when you need you?
What of the time your heart must fend for its self?

No love is strong enough that it can
decide to leave itself out of the game.

No affection can be given out there
unless it is first given in here.

Let go of the fear and what is left
will feed you and all that you cherish.

So dream of a love that leaves nothing
out, that includes your whole body and

makes miracles matter even more, from where
they aren't to where they are and must be.

THIS IS NOT ADVICE

I have witnessed the hottest fire
kindled from your heart's desires.
I have scrambled with you

across myriad fields following
dreams so readily described
but somehow lost before known.

I have seen the stutters too, the
pulling back of unfinished journeys,
the toll of so many dreams deferred.

Therefore the path you've made
is not easy, though I have felt
the groundswell strength

of your minds eye and the power
too of your knowing something different
that could have one day been true.

But it is not too late to dance,
for finishing what is started.
For hearing the simple sigh of

a job done and done so well that
no stumble of fate can put asunder.
Start simple. Then finish, finish, finish!

A GLIMPSE

Sometimes suddenly it's all different,

the way is no longer the way.

What we once saw now only shadows,

dancing on the walls we thought were real

that kept us safe from what is truely safe.

But then sometimes the heart emits one

true sound and then what we know

simply melts into how we feel.

A glimpse. A twang. A sudden

stepping into the self just beyond.

Standing on the only solid ground

that ever was. Go there now, Love

with me, with you, with us.

A WAGER

I'll bet a lot of money on this.
Jesus would just
as likely have tossed
stones at the beggars,
condemned the prostitutes,
played poker with the
Pharaoh and snorted cocaine
with the junkies at the well,
sold fake Rolex
watches to the passing
Roman soldiers, as be a
member of some of these
narrow little places
we call churches today.

THERE IS NO ACCOUNTING FOR THIS

People say, there is no accounting for taste. Well yes
that's true and we can just as easily say there is none
for leadership, Inspiration or motivation either. You see,

accounting needs things to count. The squiggles of life
made into the straight lines of no doubts, no exceptions.
Turning the juiciest of questions into dry-bone answers.

But what about love? Passion? Or a life well lived?
What about laughter, a kiss at midnight or just before?
People say, there is no accounting for this and they're right.

GOOD POEMS

There is much we cannot say about a good poem. If we could say it at all, then perhaps those words would be the poem – not the poem. We can at times, track them for brief periods through the entranced, tangled, terrain of our younger eyes. Then in an instant, we are left with a type of false indication, clearly marking the path the poem did not take. The disappearance of which works like the absence of some haunting train whistle, so lonely and hurtful that it's easily, or even, forcefully forgotten. Great lines of poetry will always beguile us, leaving at least some faint scent. A fine and timeless poem never tires of this pursuit, though we soon do and fall away, exhausted in the face of such delight. Good poems travel in summer upon the white veins of lightening, and love the malleable grasses of the forest, leaving always areas of pressed green along the way. The really exquisite poems simply lie near our bodies like old lovers and ache. In a short time they explode inside a place not unlike the heart or even in some deeper tunnel. Then a thing unseen before, not even imagined – rears its great feathered head, beats wild wings toward the silence of some vast and distant sun.

LETTER TO "J"

After all these years of fighting and ceremonies, old men burning
incense in brass pots, I'm really quite certain you could have
done it different back then if you wanted. A small tweak in
destiny, the appointment of a new saint perhaps. I know, for
example, that one slight shrug from your sad shoulder while
on that terrible cross, a slight flick of your holy wrist, even a
frown might have sent those rough soldiers flying through the
air. Those nails, that horrible hammer, all rendered useless,
leaving your sweet palms untouched. Such an amendment to
history might still have made turning the other cheek possible,
at least for a while. Hey, even heavenly patience can grow thin
over time. But listen there is one more thing I'm curious about.
That part about loving our enemies, did you really mean that?

AIKIDO

Aikido is a prayer
of movement
a poetic articulation
of the flesh.

       Always
it carries
the most sublime
possibility
the untimely
the unlikely
event
of peace.

THIS

History swerved a little today,
lost its temper,
changed its normal bearings
and decided to stage
a small hunger strike,
a kind of work

slowdown. A "to do" list
stoppage. We all waited
for hours, then days, then
months went rolling by.
But nothing at all happened?

We clenched our teeth,
we screamed, rolled on
our backs and howled
at such a miserable fate,
and all we got
for our trouble,
was this.

WINGS

On certain days
of the week, especially in winter
seagulls made clumsy by the strong winds
push inland escaping the worst of it
spinning in and out of view
just outside my window.
We both know dear reader
to apply exceptional care
when assigning intention or cause
in this or any other world.
But the gulls this morning as they burn
their great oblong shapes into the air
seem so intent on nothing in particular
as to suggest a deep and simple play
        wind under wing just for its pleasure.

I look again and the gulls have gone.
A single falcon has taken their place
and she, always the unexpected
one is all business on this day.
A fierce muscle and an iron
claw delivers her disposition toward death
slowly and ever closer to the ground.
I look again and now
the old stone crematory that shares the hill
silently burns itself back to sleep
rising from its tall brick chimney

a single spiraling sentence
slowly spoken into the air,
into the clear, bright air again and again.
Oh gentle and easy traveler,

someone is rising upon new wings
      and now you are gone.

LET ME BE HAPPY

Let me be as happy and dumb as needed
Like stars are dumb, rock lighting spinning rock
While God lays low, hushed and stunned
Don't keep me from that dog life love
Don't follow my dreams with that barking no,
That promise of an old railroad track bone that's
Hidden so deep down that even the creek can't find
It under the timbers and the creosote burning.

And you can save that old one eyed thanks too.
It sounds good but never delivers the real sweetness
Let me roam now free to be wrong in any belief
Let me sing that other song that good citizens ignore
To be let in scratchy at the back door arching for good
That old sticking screen that never opened easy but always
Swung the same right way - how happy to be as puzzled
As all the others are wrong and to wag when they growl.

MUTUAL ARISING

"I don't want to be a product of my environment.
I want my environment to be a product of me."
– Frank Costello

Reality to Frank: Sorry!
This is a dance you
can't help doing,
but that you can
learn to do just
a little better.
So listen Frank,
there is strange
and good news here:
You're not the cause, but
you're not the effect either!

THE RUTHLESS ONE

When it comes to poems,
I read fast or not at all. I sprawl
luxurious with their sounds.

I scan similes, make metaphors
slam into beautiful brick walls.
I throw flat white stones

at the speed of lightness,
across waters of which
the poet lingered long.

I bleed when words cut.
I heal when they heal.
I am the ruthless one.

And so when it comes
to what a poem means,
I mean that too.

I LOVE SHORT POEMS!

I love short poems!
They sing sudden.
They dazzle dance,
or not at all.
They're benign kamikazes,
snowflakes greeting warm
windshields then dying.
Lives being just averagely
on fire, leaves falling so
fast while sunsets blink
beautiful then vanish.
Oh yes, I love me
some short poems.
They mean quick
or not at all.

LET ME BE FAMOUS

Let me be famous.
Let me say things
more right than true,
wild and provocative,
as crazy as *loving your*
enemies. As preposterous
as *turning the other cheek*
or just saying *this is enough!*
You know none of it is true:
The way flying wasn't true, the
way we thought sound traveled
in small white pockets of rain.
The way love can never
prevail, but somehow will.

TO DAD AT 95

All you need to do now,
is just the best you can.
Of course this world is
bigger because of you.

And the world, it laughs a
little louder because of you.
The web you've weaved
has now weaved you back.

Smile. Laugh. Repeat.
The way God puts it,
"We could not have
done it without you."

And where ever it
is you go, a piece
of us will go
there too.

CROWD INSPIRED

This is for all those who somehow know
they'll get through it. For those who know
that down and out will soon be up and in.

This is for all those who have decided to
stick together and thrive, to speed the
inevitable, to be inspired and inspiring.

To be the big change by changing the big view.
To be grateful for the strength of a common vision,
and the healing touch of being community-seen.

DALE BIRON – A BIO
Coach, Poet, Speaker

*It's high time poetry came tumbling down. To the crowds,
to the folks I mean.* – Dale Biron

Dale grew up in the Piedmont region of North Carolina to a
mother who loved Latin, literature and poetry. He received his
degree from the University of North Carolina at Charlotte.
For the last two decades, he has worked with hundreds of
leaders, teams and entrepreneurs as a coach, confidant and
mentor, often serving up great poetry as a tool for awareness,
creativity and insight building.

Dale has been writing poetry for more than two decades, and
has shared his poetry and poetry-inspired presentations at such
venues as TEDx Marin, The Herbst Theatre in San Francisco,
Marin Jewish Community Center, The Center for Attitudinal
Healing, various political rallies and a host of business
conferences. He is past Poetry Editor for Gratefulness.org
and a former board member of the Marin Poetry Center. Dale
teaches poetry-based courses at The Osher Lifelong Learning
Institute at Dominican University in San Rafael, California.

Dales lives in the San Francisco Bay Area with his wife Judy
and menagerie of animals. He finds inspiration hiking the
beautiful hills and open spaces of the Golden Gate National
Recreation Area.

10496628R00079

Made in the USA
San Bernardino, CA
17 April 2014